Usborne Castles
Picture Book

Dr. Abigail Wheatley & Rachel Firth

Illustrated by Ian McNee

Designed by Tom Lalonde,
Jessica Johnson &
Stephen Moncrieff

Contents

UNDER ATTACK

round 500 years ago, during the Middle Ages, Europe was a dangerous place. Wars raged as rival lords fought each other to control the land where they lived. They wanted strong places to live. So, they built castles – strong towers surrounded by walls and ditches.

ATTACKING A CASTLE

This medieval painting (which means it's from the Middle Ages) shows an attack. The attackers are shooting arrows. But if they wanted to get into a castle, they needed heavy-duty equipment.

A *siege tower* was a wooden tower on wheels. Attackers wheeled it against a castle wall and climbed up inside it. Then, they could cross onto the top of the castle wall.

Siege tower

This is a type of catapult, known as a *trebuchet*. It was powered by a heavy weight.

Arm

Weight

Stone

Sling

When the weight was released, it pulled the arm up quickly, shooting a stone out of the sling. This could do a lot of damage to castle walls.

Attackers also tried to bring down castle walls from beneath. This picture shows attackers hiding under a wooden shelter with wheels, while they hack at the base of a tower, using picks.

TRANSPORT

Transporting siege towers and trebuchets to a castle was hard work. But there were huge amounts of other supplies – weapons, tools, arrows, food and tents. This painting shows army supplies being loaded onto ships.

Archers had a vital role. They tried to shoot anyone standing on the castle walls. Some used ordinary bows and arrows. Others used crossbows that fired short, heavy missiles, known as bolts or quarrels.

This is a crossbow. To fire it, an archer pulled the long trigger attached to the handle.

Archers often sheltered behind wooden screens, to keep them safe from defenders' arrows.

Attacking troops had to bring their own tents to live in. This was alright in fine weather, but it could be miserable if it was very cold or wet.

Food was cooked on camp fires. Wealthier knights brought servants to prepare their food and tidy their tents.

BIG GUNS

Around 1270, guns started to be used instead of trebuchets and siege towers. By around 1420, there were big guns that could smash a castle wall to pieces.

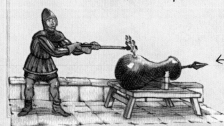

Early guns fired big, pointed bolts.

Later guns, like this one from around 1460, shot heavy iron cannonballs.

BATTLE GEAR

Knights were fighters on horseback, who played a vital part in castle warfare. To help to keep them safe, they wore tough protective clothing made from metal.

METAL SUITS

From around the year 1200, knights wore clothing made up of linked metal rings, known as *chain mail*. On top, they wore a linen tunic and a helmet made from metal plates.

Close up, chain mail looked like this. It was difficult and expensive to make, as each tiny ring was made by hand and then fastened to other rings.

From 1450, knights were covered from head to toe in suits made from metal plates.

From around 1350, knights were wearing metal plates on top of their chain mail. This suit has a helmet, breastplate and arm, leg, hand and foot guards, all made from metal plates.

Chain mail could quickly get rusty. Trainee knights, called squires, rubbed it with sand to take the rust off.

HELMETS

Some helmets protected just the top of the head, while others covered the face, too, with holes for seeing and breathing.

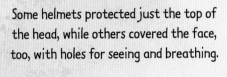

Helmets like this one were called *armets* and were in use around 1450.

This style of helmet dates from around 1050. It was often worn over a chain mail hood.

This helmet, known as a *great helm*, was worn around 1370. It has a slit to see through and lots of holes to make breathing easier.

The front, pointed section is hinged, so the knight could lift it up if he wanted to see more.

SAFE BUT AWKWARD

Metal clothing was good for protection, but it was very heavy and restricted knights' movements. They needed a lot of help to get it on and off.

Many knights wore hand-protectors, known as *gauntlets*. But they made it difficult to move the fingers easily.

If a knight's battle gear had been dented during fighting, he might need a blacksmith to hammer it back into shape before he could take it off.

Foot-protectors were known as *sabatons*. They had overlapping plates to make them flex, but they were *still* hard to walk in.

A full suit of battle gear was very heavy. But it was even heavier for the poor horse, who had to carry the knight.

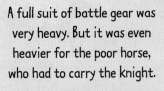

WEAPONS

As well as protective clothing, knights needed weapons to fight off their enemies. Every knight had a sword, but there were plenty of other weapons that could be useful in hand-to-hand fighting, too.

BLADES AND LANCES

Swords were very versatile, as knights could use them on horseback or on foot. They varied in shape and size as fashions changed.

This sword dates from around 1350-1400. The part above the blade is known as the *hilt*.

Swordbelt

Dagger

Scabbard

A knight kept his sword on a belt, in a leather case or *scabbard*. He also had a dagger, with its own scabbard.

This long, pointed wooden weapon is called a *lance*. Knights used lances when fighting on horseback, to spear each other, or push each other to the ground.

Point

Edge

A knight used the point of his sword for stabbing, and two sharp edges for slashing.

This sword dates from around 1480. It belonged to King Francis I of France.

Couched lance

A knight held his lance clamped or *couched* firmly under his right arm.

SHIELDS

Knights carried wood and leather shields, to fend off their enemies' weapons. Early shields were large, but later designs were smaller as protective clothing became more effective.

Early shields were shaped like this, and covered a knight from his chin to his knees.

In an emergency, a knight could use his shield to hit out.

Later, knights used shields like this one, to protect the area from the shoulder to the waist.

HAFTED WEAPONS

Knights also had weapons with medium-length handles, known as *hafts*. These could be used for fighting both on horseback and on foot.

This spiky metal club is a *mace*. It was used to deliver crushing blows.

This is a war hammer. A blow from it could crush metal plates.

Battle-axes like this were sometimes decorated with engraved patterns.

Mace

War hammer

Knights often kept a hafted weapon hanging by their saddle, in case they lost their sword.

In an emergency, knights could throw battle-axes at their enemies.

HORSES

Without their trusty steeds, knights wouldn't have gone far. In fact, horses were so vital that every castle had a stable and servants, called grooms, to look after the horses.

WAR HORSES

Every knight had a war horse, known as a *steed*, or *destrier*. In battle, steeds wore protective coverings. At first, these were made from padded cloth, leather or chain mail, with a leather face protector.

Later, steeds wore metal plate coverings. These had a chest protector or *peytral*, and a rear protector, or *crupper*.

Packhorse

Steed

Steeds were hugely expensive and hard to train. Knights had other, less costly horses for ordinary riding and for carrying baggage.

Riding horse

A steed's face protector was known as a *shaffron*. This one, decorated with gold, was made for the horse of King Henry VIII of England, in around 1540.

Although battles could be dangerous for horses, it was definitely 'against the rules' for a knight to harm a steed deliberately.

RIDING HORSES

Smaller, lighter horses were used for everyday riding. Some were specially bred to have a smooth way of walking that made them comfortable to ride, even on long journeys.

Riding horses wore leather harnesses. Some were richly decorated, like these. The patterns come from coats of arms (pages 10-11).

Horseshoe

Farrier

All horses wore metal shoes to protect their feet during long rides. The shoes were made and fitted by *farriers*.

Riding saddles were often beautifully decorated. This one has been carved and painted with elaborate designs.

From around the year 1350, it became popular for ladies to sit sideways on specially designed saddles known as *sidesaddles*.

Lady riding sidesaddle

Some grand ladies rode in horse-drawn carriages.

SPURS

Spurs like this were attached to a rider's feet, and used to encourage the horse to move faster.

Spurs

Spurs were thought so important that, when a man became a knight, he was given a new pair of spurs as part of a formal ceremony.

New knight

COATS OF ARMS

oats of arms were painted on knights' shields, so people could see who was who in a battle. Each knightly family had its own design, drawn up according to strict rules, known as heraldry.

THE RULES OF HERALDRY

Each part of a coat of arms has a name.

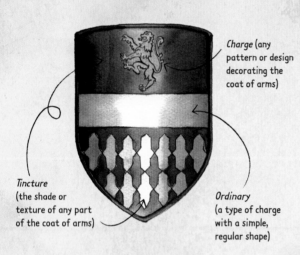

Charge (any pattern or design decorating the coat of arms)

Tincture (the shade or texture of any part of the coat of arms)

Ordinary (a type of charge with a simple, regular shape)

TINCTURES

Azure (blue)

Gules (red)

Sable (black)

Vert (green)

Or (gold)

Argent (silver)

Ermine (stoat fur texture)

Vair (squirrel fur texture)

CHARGES

Portcullis (castle gate)

Escallop (shell)

Lion rampant (standing lion)

Fleur de lys (lily flower)

Mullet (star)

Martlet (small bird)

ORDINARIES

Chief

Saltire

Cross

Fess

Chevron

Pale

Bend

Pile

SHOWING OFF

At first, knights displayed coats of arms on their shields. Later, they wore them on every part of their battle gear.

This Italian knight has a coat of arms featuring gold lily flowers on a red background.

If one knightly family was related to another, they might display their coats of arms together.

These carved wooden animals are holding the coats of arms of two different families.

This coat of arms is part of a stained glass window. A knight paid for it to decorate a window in his local church.

Banner

Tunic

Window

Knights sometimes used their coats of arms to decorate clothing, furnishings, and even buildings.

HERALDS

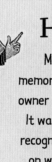

Men called *heralds* memorized the name of the owner of each coat of arms. It was the herald's job to recognize who was fighting on which side in battles.

After important battles or tournaments, heralds made lists to record every knight who had taken part.

Heralds

Coats of arms and heralds still exist today. This modern herald's tunic is decorated with the British royal coat of arms.

Modern heralds design coats of arms and announce important events, such as the coronation of new kings or queens.

11

INSIDE A CASTLE

It's easy to imagine castles as bare, gloomy places. But inside, rooms were often filled with elegant furniture and lavish ornaments, with walls decorated with painted designs and wall hangings.

LIFE OF LUXURY

This painted scene from a medieval book shows wealthy ladies reclining on soft cushions in a comfortable bedroom with hangings on the walls.

Stone floors could be chilly, so dried rushes were scattered over them, and swept up when they were dirty. Other coverings included rush mats, fur rugs and floor tiles.

Castle windows let in enough light to see by day. At night, flaming torches and candles were lit. Many castles had built-in shelves for candlesticks to stand on.

This floor tile is decorated with patterns and a picture of an English king, Richard I, on horseback.

Clothes, books and other things were kept in boxes and chests. Some, like this one, were decorated with paintings.

DECORATION

Bare stone walls were often painted with bright patterns and pictures, or hung with painted ornaments carved from wood or stone.

This carved stone shield was made to be hung inside.

Walls were also hung with tapestries, like this one showing a lord and lady relaxing in a forest glade.

Castle owners brought luxurious ornaments home from their travels. This decorated drinking glass was brought back from Syria by a Crusader knight (see pages 24-25).

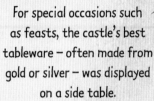

For special occasions such as feasts, the castle's best tableware – often made from gold or silver – was displayed on a side table.

CASTLE CHAPEL

The castle chapel was where religious ceremonies were held. It was often richly decorated.

This gold and silver cross would have been displayed where everyone could see it.

Sometimes, the lord of the castle sat in a private room off the chapel, away from everyone else. There was a window through to the chapel, so he could see the service taking place.

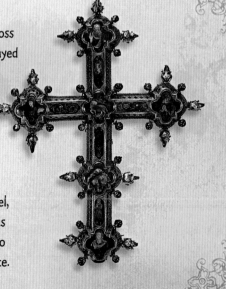

13

FEASTING

Every castle had a great hall for holding feasts to celebrate special occasions such as religious festivals. The castle cooks were busy for days before a feast, preparing food for all the guests.

FOOD

Many castles had gardens, orchards, farms and fishponds, to provide food for the castle kitchens. The cooks had to plan the feast according to what was available at that time of year.

Most fruits and vegetables had to be used right away, as there was no way of keeping them fresh.

Fishing

Wild food – including deer, boar and some types of fish – was caught for feasts.

CASTLE KITCHENS

Castles had huge kitchens where armies of cooks worked around the clock, preparing and cooking food and making elaborate sauces and decorations.

Herbs and spices were often ground into a powder or paste and mixed into sauces.

Grinding spices

Huge cauldrons like this one were used for boiling up soups and stews. Sometimes there was a separate room for cauldrons, known as the *boiling room*.

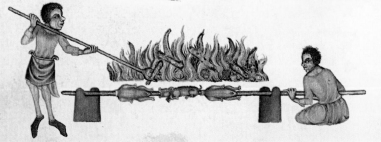

Meat was threaded onto metal poles called *spits* and roasted in front of huge fires. Boys turned the spits, to make sure the meat cooked all over.

AT THE TABLE

The feast was served in the great hall, on big tables laid with white tablecloths. The lord sat with his family and close friends on a raised platform, at a separate table known as the *high table*.

Roast boar's head

Roast peacock

Some dishes for feasts were very elaborate. Roast peacocks had their feathers stuck back on, to make them look as lifelike as possible.

Diners drank from cups or *goblets*. The most expensive ones were made from silver or gold. This gold cup has designs made from enamel.

Wine cup

Butler

Drinks were served by a butler and his team of servants. They poured out ale and different kinds of wine and carried the cups to the diners.

Hardly anyone used forks, but guests brought their own knives and spoons. Instead of plates, people cut their food on square platters called *trenchers*, made from metal, wood, or stale bread.

Trencher

This big knife was for carving meat. The small ones were used for eating.

There was always plenty of food left over after a grand feast. This medieval painting shows food being given to a poor person at a castle gate.

FUN AND GAMES

Even in peacetime, castles were bustling places. There were sporting tournaments, hunts in nearby forests, and pastimes such as games and music.

TOURNAMENTS

Lords often held tournaments at their castles. These were contests where knights fought mock battles to see who was the most skilled. Sometimes, tournaments lasted for days, with feasting every night.

Jousting was the part of a tournament where two knights tried to knock each other off their horses.

Tournaments could be very dangerous. Some knights were badly injured, or even killed.

Injured knight

Protective gear was made especially for tournaments. This metal suit was for a part of a tournament where knights fought on foot with weapons called *poleaxes*.

This decorative shield, adorned with gold, was a tournament prize, awarded to the knight who had shown the most skill.

For tournaments, knights often draped their helmets with cloth known as *mantling*, topped with elaborate decorations called *crests*.

Winner

Prize

Crest

Mantling

An important lady usually presented the prize to the winner.

PASTIMES

In spare moments, knights and their ladies might dance, play music or board games, listen to poets reading out their work, or watch jesters play the fool.

This painting shows a couple sitting in a garden playing a board game similar to backgammon. Chess was another popular board game in castle times.

Jesters told jokes, leaped around and made silly noises to entertain people.

Knights learned to play musical instruments, such as this *rebec*.

HUNTING

Lords, knights and ladies liked to go hunting. They rode into the forest chasing deer, wild boar, bears or foxes. They took trained hunting dogs with them, to sniff out the prey.

Hunters called to each other, using hunting horns, like this one.

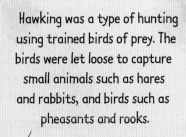

A hunt could be over quickly or take all day, depending on how quick and clever the hunted animal was.

Hawking was a type of hunting using trained birds of prey. The birds were let loose to capture small animals such as hares and rabbits, and birds such as pheasants and rooks.

Hungry hunters sometimes stopped for a rest and a picnic.

Hawk

CASTLE TREASURE

Most castles had a strong room, where the lord's valuables were kept under lock and key. Treasures might include jewels, coins and gold goblets, religious ornaments and, sometimes, a crown encrusted with gems.

JEWELS

For safe keeping, jewels were often stored in boxes known as *caskets*.

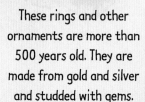

These rings and other ornaments are more than 500 years old. They are made from gold and silver and studded with gems.

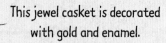

This jewel casket is decorated with gold and enamel.

Wearing expensive jewels was a way for wealthy men and women to show how important they were.

GOBLETS

Richly decorated goblets might be used for religious ceremonies, as well as for drinking.

This gold, lidded goblet, decorated with pictures made from enamel, was given to the King of France by a French nobleman.

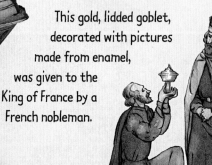

This one is made from gold, jewels and agate – a decorative stone.

CROWNS

Crowns came in different shapes and sizes, and they were often encrusted with dazzling jewels.

This gold and silver crown, adorned with angels, was made for Louis IX, King of France.

An English noblewoman named Margaret had this crown made for her wedding in 1468.

German kings and emperors wore this gold crown, decorated with pearls, emeralds, sapphires, amethysts and a large cross.

This gold crown, set with sapphires, rubies, diamonds and pearls, was made for a queen.

RELIGIOUS ORNAMENTS

Costly ornaments were used in religious ceremonies, or to decorate churches or castle chapels.

This golden ornament, called a *censer*, was used for burning fragrant incense during religious services.

The censer was swung gently on its chain, to waft the smell of incense around.

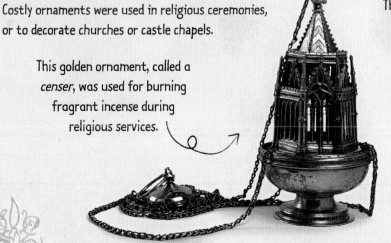

THE FIRST CASTLES

The first castles were built in Europe around a thousand years ago. Many were made from wood and earth and were fairly small and basic. But stone castles soon caught on and, over the next few centuries, they became much bigger and stronger and were built in many different shapes and sizes.

AROUND 1070

Early castles were often made by digging deep ditches and piling the earth up. Buildings were surrounded by wooden fences, with a tall tower where guards kept watch. Some towers were put on a high earth mound, called a *motte*.

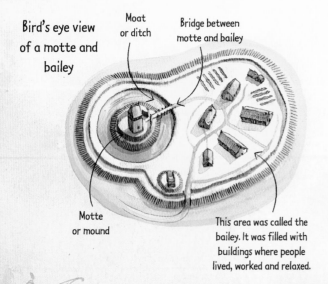

Bird's eye view of a motte and bailey

Moat or ditch

Bridge between motte and bailey

Motte or mound

This area was called the bailey. It was filled with buildings where people lived, worked and relaxed.

A reconstruction of an early castle, Lütjenburg, Germany

All the earth had to be shifted by workers using shovels. Sometimes hundreds of workers were used, so it would be finished quickly.

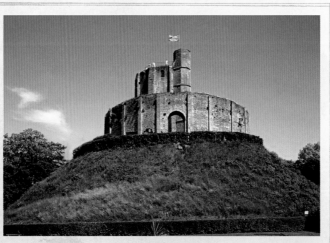

Gisors Castle, France, begun in the 1090s

This motte was built in 1097. The stone buildings were begun in the 1170s.

Timber was quick and easy to build with, but stone was stronger and lasted longer. So lords eventually replaced timber towers with stone ones. But many mottes were too soft to support stone buildings, so mottes went out of fashion.

AROUND 1170

Early stone castles often had a huge tower, or *keep*, surrounded by banks and ditches topped by stone walls. If enemies got through the outer walls, everyone rushed into the keep for protection.

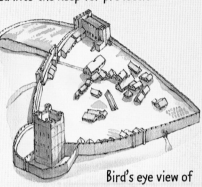

This keep was built around 1140 -1170.

Bird's eye view of Richmond Castle

Richmond Castle, England, begun in 1071

AROUND 1200

Over time, lords built keeps in all kinds of different shapes. Rounded keeps became popular for a while, as the smooth walls were harder to attack.

This round tower has been cut away, so you can see the rooms inside.

This round tower was built in 1207.

Falaise Castle, France, begun in the 1120s

AROUND 1240

More complicated shapes soon caught on, too. The space inside could easily be divided up into more comfortable, smaller rooms for eating, sleeping or relaxing. By now, lords demanded comfort as well as security.

Del Monte Castle, Italy, built around 1240-50

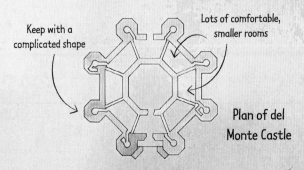

Keep with a complicated shape

Lots of comfortable, smaller rooms

Plan of del Monte Castle

LATER CASTLES

s the centuries passed, castles became more and more popular. They were also grander and much more comfortable to live in.

AROUND 1280

Over time, castles were designed to be stronger and stronger. Tall inner walls loomed over shorter outer ones, so archers could fire from the tops of both walls at once. Sometimes, the keep was placed over the castle gate, guarding the entrance to the castle.

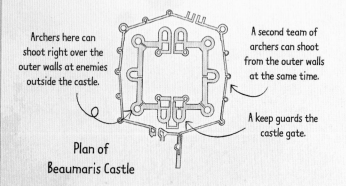

Archers here can shoot right over the outer walls at enemies outside the castle.

A second team of archers can shoot from the outer walls at the same time.

A keep guards the castle gate.

Plan of Beaumaris Castle

Beaumaris Castle, Wales, begun in 1295 but never completed

How Beaumaris Castle might have looked if it had been finished

AROUND 1380

By now, castles still had to be big and strong. But they were also built to be as beautiful and comfortable as possible, with fireplaces in every bedroom, separate toilet facilities, elegant carvings on the stonework and some big windows to let in lots of light.

Kwidzyn Castle, Poland, completed around 1380-90

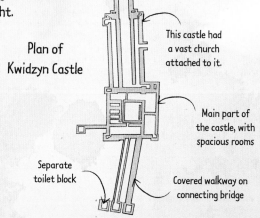

Plan of Kwidzyn Castle

This castle had a vast church attached to it.

Main part of the castle, with spacious rooms

Separate toilet block

Covered walkway on connecting bridge

This castle was built from bricks. Brick castles were often built in places where building stone was hard to find.

Castle of Manzanares el Real, Spain, begun in 1475

AROUND 1470

Armies were now using cannons that could blast castle walls apart. But lords still wanted to live in impressive castles, fitted with modern luxuries. These castles weren't necessarily that strong, but they looked so forbidding that they made enemies think twice about attacking.

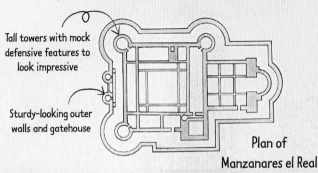

Tall towers with mock defensive features to look impressive

Sturdy-looking outer walls and gatehouse

Plan of Manzanares el Real

AROUND 1540

Some small, low castles with very thick walls were specially built to fire cannon from. (Tall castle walls would have cracked from the shock of the blast.)
However, these small castles weren't very grand, so lords often built palaces for living in instead.

How Deal Castle would have looked with cannon in place

Deal Castle, England, built in 1539

LATER CASTLES

Centuries after castles stopped being safe places to live, some people still love the idea of living in one. This one was built by a king and fitted with modern luxuries, including bathrooms, central heating and electricity.

Neuschwanstein Castle, Germany, begun in 1869

CRUSADE CASTLES

The Crusades were bitter religious wars fought between Christians and Muslims, which started in 1095 and continued for hundreds of years. Both sides built castles to keep themselves and their territories safe.

The Crusades began when Christians known as *crusaders* invaded parts of the Middle East to attack Muslims who had recently settled there. The crusaders had a long journey to get there, often in ships.

When crusaders first arrived, they had to live in tents. But they soon built castles, where they could live in more comfort and safety.

Some crusaders captured castles from the Muslims. Sometimes, castles changed hands again and again. This painting shows crusaders attacking a Muslim fortress in 1199.

Christians fought Crusades against Muslims in Spain and Portugal, too. Impressive crusade castles were built there, often with splendid gardens.

RELIGIOUS ORDERS

Some crusader knights joined groups known as religious orders. They took vows like monks, but fought and built castles.

The Teutonic Knights belonged to a German religious order. They fought Crusades in Eastern Europe to force local followers of Pagan religions to become Christians. They built Kwidzyn Castle (page 22) and Malbork Castle (page 29) in Poland.

In this painting, a crusader is wearing a red cross to show he is one of the Knights Templar. This religious order built many castles in the Middle East, including Tortosa and Chastel Rouge, marked on the map opposite.

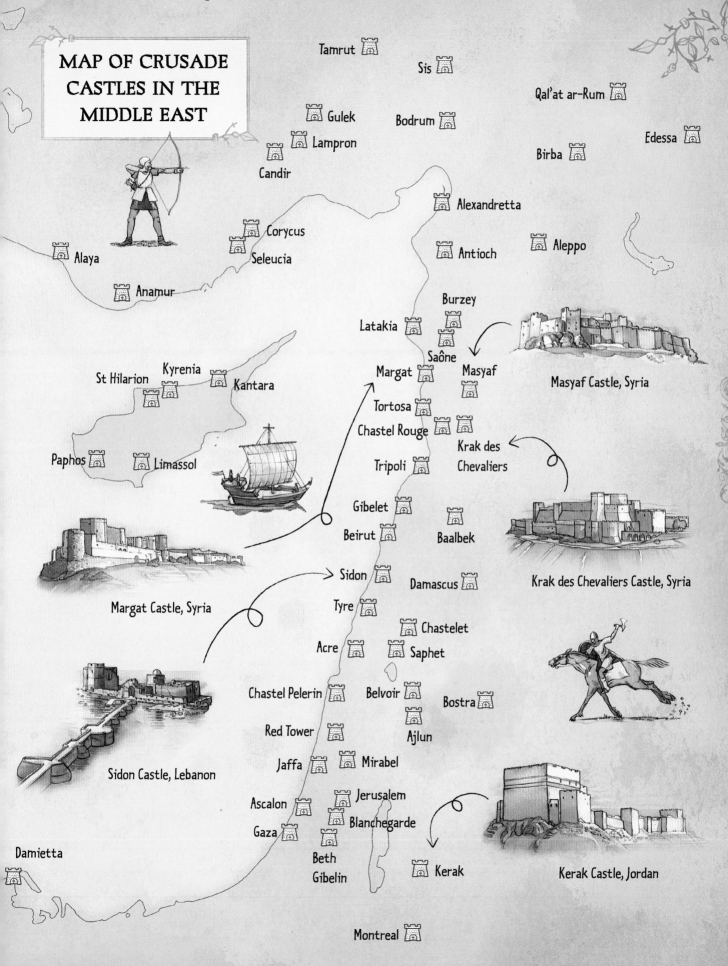

MAP OF CRUSADE CASTLES IN THE MIDDLE EAST

Tamrut

Sis

Qal'at ar-Rum

Gulek

Bodrum

Edessa

Lampron

Birba

Candir

Alexandretta

Corycus

Antioch

Aleppo

Alaya

Seleucia

Anamur

Burzey

Latakia

Saône

Masyaf

St Hilarion

Kyrenia

Margat

Masyaf Castle, Syria

Kantara

Tortosa

Chastel Rouge

Krak des
Chevaliers

Paphos

Limassol

Tripoli

Gibelet

Beirut

Baalbek

Krak des Chevaliers Castle, Syria

Sidon

Damascus

Tyre

Margat Castle, Syria

Chastelet

Acre

Saphet

Chastel Pelerin

Belvoir

Bostra

Red Tower

Ajlun

Jaffa

Mirabel

Sidon Castle, Lebanon

Ascalon

Jerusalem

Gaza

Blanchegarde

Damietta

Beth
Gibelin

Kerak

Kerak Castle, Jordan

Montreal

25

FAMOUS CASTLES

Since castle times, many castles have crumbled away or been knocked down, but some are still standing, and a few are even lived in. Here are some of the most famous ones. You'll also find them marked on the map on page 25, or on pages 30-31.

THE TOWER OF LONDON, ENGLAND

Building started at the Tower of London in 1078. It was used as a royal home, but also became infamous as a place where important people were imprisoned and executed. Since 1485, the Tower has been guarded by soldiers known as Yeoman Warders, or Beefeaters.

This Yeoman Warder takes care of the Tower's ravens – birds that are thought to bring good luck to the castle.

ALHAMBRA, SPAIN

The name Alhambra comes from the Arabic title, *qa'lat al-Hamra'*, meaning *red castle*, after the reddish stone the castle is built from. Most of the present castle dates from the 1330s to the 1390s, and includes beautiful gardens, courtyards, elaborate carved stonework and bright, patterned tiles. It was built by a Muslim family known as the Nasrids, who ruled southern Spain for 200 years.

A tiled section of the Alhambra

PIERREFONDS CASTLE, FRANCE

Pierrefonds was begun in 1393, but it was damaged during fighting around 1619 and remained a romantic ruin for centuries. Between 1857 and 1885, there was a vast project to rebuild the castle, led by a famous architect, Viollet le Duc. He designed many details from his imagination, so the modern castle is different from the original one.

Pierrefonds Castle when it was still in ruins, around 1800

ELTZ CASTLE, GERMANY

Standing on a crag, Eltz castle is surrounded on three sides by the River Eltz. In 1268, the owners divided the castle, giving each part of the family their own section of the castle to live in. Arranged around a central courtyard, the castle was built between the 1150s and the 1660s, though it was heavily restored between 1845 and 1888.

The same family has owned Eltz for more than 800 years. This is a coat of arms belonging to one branch of the family.

EDINBURGH CASTLE, SCOTLAND

Edinburgh Castle stands on a huge cliff known as Castle Rock. The earliest part dates from 1130. The castle houses the Honours of Scotland – Scotland's royal crown, sceptre and sword – along with the Stone of Destiny, on which Scottish monarchs sat when they were crowned.

Stone of Destiny

Sword

Sceptre

Crown

MORE FAMOUS CASTLES

CAERNARFON CASTLE, WALES

With its angular towers and pale walls striped with narrow bands of darker stone, Caernarfon Castle has a very distinctive look. Built at the mouth of the River Seiont between 1283 and 1330, it has two huge gates, and a small water gate for people arriving by boat.

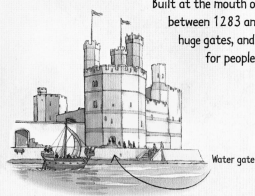

Water gate

KRAK DES CHEVALIERS CASTLE, SYRIA

Originally built by local people, this castle was conquered during the Crusades by religious knights called Hospitallers. The knights rebuilt and added to the castle, making it one of the strongest in the area. It withstood many sieges until Muslim fighters eventually conquered it in 1271.

CASTEL SANT'ANGELO, ITALY

Castel Sant'Angelo stands next to the Tiber, the main river of the city of Rome. It is arranged around a vast, round tower which was originally built in Roman times as a tomb for the Emperor Hadrian.

The castle's name comes from a legend that an angel was once seen on top of the building.

BRAN CASTLE, ROMANIA

Bran Castle is situated on a steep, rocky crag on the borders of a mountainous area known as Transylvania. The present castle was begun in 1377, and was used to control routes through the nearby mountains. For a short period it was owned by Vlad III, a local ruler notorious for his cruelty.

Bran Castle, along with other castles in the area, may have inspired Dracula's castle in stories about the fictional vampire, Count Dracula.

KARLŠTEJN CASTLE, CZECH REPUBLIC

Karlštejn Castle was begun in 1348, to provide a safe place to keep the priceless crown jewels of the local rulers. The most imposing part of the castle is a tall rectangular tower, which contains the chapel where the jewels were kept for around 200 years. The chapel itself is decorated with portraits of Czech kings painted around the year 1360.

The chapel of Karlštejn Castle

MALBORK CASTLE, POLAND

Malbork is a red brick castle built by the Teutonic Knights (see page 24). Begun around 1276, it expanded until, by 1406, it could house 3,000 knights. It consists of three enclosures surrounded by a vast wall. Inside are workshops, a monastery and a grand residence for the head Teutonic Knight – the Grand Master.

The Grand Master's residence, Malbork Castle

CASTLES IN EUROPE

T his map shows some of the more important castles that survive in Europe today.

Blarney Castle, Ireland

Gravensteen Castle, Holland

Saumur Castle, France

Guimarães Castle, Portugal

Duffus
Kildrummy
Castle Sween
Stirling
Edinburgh
Carrickfergus
Alnwick
Warkworth
Caerlaverock
Threave
Richmond
Roscommon
Trim
Caernarfon
Conisborough
Nenagh
Blarney
Castell y Bere
Kenilworth
Norwich
Warwick
Framlingham
Mui
Pembroke
Cardiff
Loeve
Portchester
London
Launceston
Dover
Gravensteen
Corfe Castle
Be
Pierrefonds
Caen
Gisors
Falaise
Vincennes
Fougères
Domfront
Angers
Amboise
Saumur
Châteauneuf
Niort
Culan
La Brède
Montfort
Bonaguil
Pau
Tarasco
Olite
Foix
Bragança
Carcassonne
Guimarães
Peñafiel
Coca
Segovia
Leiria
Manzanares el Real
Montalbán
Belmonte
Elvas
Beja
Calatrava la Nueva
Monteagudo
Alcalá de Guadaíra
Bellver
Silves
Granada
Málaga

30

enhus/
resborg
Akershus
Bohus
Helsingborg
Kronborg
Egeskov
Malmö
Nyborg
Glücksburg
Gottorf
Kalmar
Hammershus
Spandau
Moritzburg
Wartburg
Grodziec
Chojnik
Karlštejn
Hukvaldy
Będzin
Wawel
Niedzica
Lutsk
Olesko
Eltz
Starkenburg
Nuremberg
Heidelberg
Zvíkov
Orava
Spiš
Palanok
Khotyn
Kamyanets-Podilsky
Lichtenstein
Burghausen
Linz
Dürnstein
Salzburg
Bratislava
Bojnice
Salgó
Sárospatak
Esztergom
Buda
Soyhières
Neuschwanstein
Hochosterwitz
Simontornya
Tarasp
Velenje
Veliki Tabor
Misox
Castelvecchio
Branik
Trakošćan
Bač
Vršac
Hunyad
Bran
Castello
Visconteo
Castello di
San Giorgio
Trsat
Frankopan
Jajce
Doboj
Golubac
Baba Vida
Malaspina
Mirabella
Bijela
Tabija
Koznik
Tsarevets
Castel Sismondo
Rocca
Maggiore
Castello Spagnolo
Kotor
Markovi Kuli
Asenova
krepost
Castel
Sant'Angelo
Lucera
Carski Kuli
Krujë
Castel Nuovo
Castel del Monte
Berat
Kastro
Larissa
Angelokastro
Castello di
Lombardia
Castello Ursino
Chlemoutsi
Palaiokastro
Bourtzi
Bodrum
Marmaris
Kos
Rhodes
Silifke
Mamure
St Hilarion
Kolossi
Frangokastello

Häme
Olavinlinna
Vyborg
Talinn
Narva/Ivangorod
Rakvere
Novgorod
Paide
Kuressaare
Turaida
Cēsis
Koknese
Riga
Kaunas
Trakai
Lida
Mir
Malbork
Gniew
Kwidzyn
Golub-Dobrzyń
Koło
Kamyanyets

Kalmar Castle, Sweden

Spiš Castle, Slovakia

Trakošćan Castle, Croatia

Bourtzi Castle, Greece

INDEX

USBORNE QUICKLINKS

For links to websites where you can find out more about castles, go to the Usborne Quicklinks website at www.usborne.com/quicklinks and type in the keywords 'Castles picture book'. Please read our internet safety guidelines at the Usborne Quicklinks website. We recommend that children are supervised while using the internet.

ACKNOWLEDGEMENTS

Every effort has been made to trace and acknowledge ownership of copyright. If any rights have been omitted, the publishers offer to rectify this in any future editions following notification. The publishers are grateful to the following individuals and organizations for their permission to reproduce material on the following pages: t=top, m=middle, b=bottom, r=right, l=left

Cover: l © Ocean/Corbis; m © Darama/Corbis; r Ms.Fr 122 f.1 Sir Lancelot crosses the Sword Bridge, from the Roman de Lancelot du Lac, 1344 (vellum), French School, (14th century) / Bibliothèque Nationale, Paris, France / The Bridgeman Art Library

p2–3 Under attack: p2t © The British Library Board; p2bl © Hemis / Alamy; p2br © The British Library Board; p3t © Sonia Halliday Photographs / Alamy; p3mr Crossbow, with a steel bow painted with red flowers, from Bavaria, c.1450-70 (mixed media) by German School, (15th century) © Wallace Collection, London, UK / The Bridgeman Art Library; p3ml © The British Library Board; p3b Photo Scala Florence/Heritage Images;

p4–5 Battle gear: p4l Model of a man at arms in Italian armour of the late 13th century (mixed media), Wroe, Peter (20th century) / Royal Armouries, Leeds, UK / The Bridgeman Art Library; p4m Model of a man at arms in Italian armour of the late 14th century (mixed media), Wroe, Peter (20th century) / Royal Armouries, Leeds, UK / The Bridgeman Art Library; p4r Suit of armour with poulaines, c.1480 (metal), French School, (15th century) / Musée de l'Armée, Paris, France / Giraudon / The Bridgeman Art Library; p5tl Great helm, c.1370 (metal), English School, (14th century) / Royal Armouries, Leeds, UK / The Bridgeman Art Library; p5tr © INTERFOTO / Alamy; p5m The Board of Trustees of the Armouries / HIP / TopFoto; p5b The Board of Trustees of the Armouries / HIP / TopFoto;

p6–7 Weapons: p6l Sword, second half of fourteenth century / © Wallace Collection, London, UK / The Bridgeman Art Library; p6m © Paris – Musée de l'Armée, Dist. RMN–Grand Palais / Pascal Segrette; p6r © Tibor Bognar/Corbis; p7tl © Victoria and Albert Museum, London; p7tr Photo: akg-images / Erich Lessing; p7bl Mace with a head with six flanges and a hexagonal haft, c.1470 (steel, copper alloy, cord and leather), German School, (15th century) / © Wallace Collection, London, UK / The Bridgeman Art Library; p7bm War hammer, with an oak haft, c.1450 (iron and oak), French School, (15th century) / © Wallace Collection, London, UK / The Bridgeman Art Library; p7br Various pikes, European, 15th-16th century (iron), © Wallace Collection, London, UK/ The Bridgeman Art Library;

p8–9 Horses: p8tl © The British Library Board; p8tr © ImageState / Alamy; p8b The Board of Trustees of the Armouries / HIP / TopFoto; p9tl © The British Library Board; p9tr © Victoria and Albert Museum, London; p9ml Saddle with a pommel, with a relief of a man and woman, c.1440-60 (wood, horn, bark, leather and wax), German School, (15th century) / © Wallace Collection, London, UK / The Bridgeman Art Library; p9mr © The British Library Board; p9b © RMN–Grand Palais (musée de Cluny – musée national du Moyen-Âge) / Jean-Gilles Berizzi;

p10–11 Coats of arms: p11tl © The British Library Board; p11tr © Victoria and Albert Museum, London; p11ml © Colin Underhill / Alamy; p11bl Initial of the Grant of Arms to John Smert, Garter King, 1450, to the Tallow Chandlers' Company 24th September, 1456, / Tallow Chandlers' Company, London, UK / The Bridgeman Art Library; p11bm © Philadelphia Museum of Art/CORBIS;

p12–13 Inside a castle: p12t © The British Library Board; p12m © The Trustees of the British Museum; p12b © The Art Archive / Alamy; p13tl © The Art Gallery Collection / Alamy; p13tr © Museum of London; p13m © Victoria and Albert Museum, London; p13b © Victoria and Albert Museum, London;

p14–15 Feasting: p14t © PRISMA ARCHIVO / Alamy; p14m © Neil Cameron / Alamy; p14b © The British Library Board; p15t © The British Library Board; p15m © The Trustees of the British Museum; p15bl © The Trustees of the British Museum; p15br © The Print Collector / Alamy;

p16–17 Fun and games: p16t © The British Library Board; p16bl Foot combat armour of King Henry VIII, 1520 (metal), English School, (16th century) / Royal Armouries, Leeds, UK / The Bridgeman Art Library; p16br © The Trustees of the British Museum; p17tl © The British Library Board; p17tr © Lebrecht Music and Arts Photo Library / Alamy; p17m © The Trustees of the British Museum; p17b © The Art Gallery Collection / Alamy;

p18–19 Castle treasure: p18t © The Trustees of the British Museum; p18bl © The Trustees of the British Museum; p18br © The Art Archive / Alamy; p19tl © ClassicStock / Alamy; p19tr © Alexei Fateev / Alamy; p19ml © The Art Gallery Collection / Alamy; p19mr Ronald Sheridan@Ancient Art & Architecture Collection Ltd.; p19b © Victoria and Albert Museum, London;

p20–21 The first castles: p20t With thanks to the curators of Turmhügelburg, Lütjenburg, Germany; p20b © Bildarchiv Monheim GmbH / Alamy; p21t © Robert Harding Picture Library Ltd / Alamy; p21m © Les. Ladbury / Alamy; p21b © LOETSCHER CHLAUS / Alamy;

p22–23 Later castles: p22t © Jason Gallier / Alamy; p22b © imagebroker / Alamy; p23t © Jerónimo Alba / Alamy; p23m © Skyscan Photolibrary / Alamy; p23b © Stock Connection Blue / Alamy;

p24–25 Crusade castles: p24t © The Art Archive / Alamy; p24m Fr 22495 f.69v The Crusader assault on Jerusalem in 1099, from Le Roman de Godefroi de Bouillon (vellum), French School, (14th century) / Bibliothèque Nationale, Paris, France / The Bridgeman Art Library; p24b © INTERFOTO / Alamy;

p26–27 Famous castles: p26t © David Ball / Alamy; p26b © Jon Arnold Images Ltd / Alamy; p27t © Hemis / Alamy; p27m © incamerastock / Alamy; p27b © Doug Houghton / Alamy;

p28–29 More famous castles: p28t © CW Images / Alamy; p28m © Peter Horree / Alamy; p28b © Ken Welsh / Alamy; p29t © wronaphoto.com / Alamy; p29m © Profimedia International s.r.o. / Alamy; p29b © Jan Wlodarczyk / Alamy

Edited by Jane Chisholm
Additional design by Emily Beevers, Samantha Barrett, Brenda Cole and Lucy Wain
With thanks to Ruth King
Digital manipulation by John Russell and Nick Wakeford